SPEAK TO THE EARTH

Appreciating and Conserving
Our Beautiful World ...
In Thoughts and Photographs

SPEAK TO THE EARTH

With Anne Morrow Lindbergh, John F. Kennedy,
William O. Douglas, Rachel Carson,
Walter Cronkite, and many more

Selected by Shifra Stein

♛ Hallmark Crown Editions

Acknowledgments

Excerpt from "The Winds That Blow the Earth" by J.A. Maxtone Graham in *American Forests Magazine*. Reprinted by permission. Excerpt by Friends of the Earth from *The Environmental Handbook*, edited by Garrett De Bell. Copyright © 1970 by Garrett De Bell. Reprinted by permission of Ballantine Books, Inc. Excerpt from *Echoes in a Conch Shell* by Hal Borland from *Audubon* Magazine. Reprinted by permission of Collins-Knowlton-Wing, Inc. Copyright © 1971, by Hal Borland. Excerpts from "Peace of Mind" by Walter Cronkite and James Michener in *Look* Magazine (July 27, 1971). Excerpt from "A Place for Snakes as Well as Naked Lovers" by George B. Leonard in *Look* Magazine (January 13, 1970). Both reprinted by permission of Cowles Communications, Inc. Excerpt from *The Long Shadowed Forest* by Helen Hoover. Copyright © 1963 by Helen Hoover. Reprinted by permission of Thomas Y. Crowell Company, Inc. Excerpt by Sir F. Fraser Darling and Noel D. Eichorn from "Man and Nature in the National Parks" from *National Parks & Conservation Magazine*. Reprinted by permission. Excerpt by Faith McNulty from *War on Wildlife* in *National Parks and Conservation Magazine* (March 1971). Reprinted by permission. Excerpt from *My Wilderness: The Pacific West*, by William O. Douglas. Copyright © 1960 by William O. Douglas. Excerpt from "Beauty in Our Own Back Yard" in *Love and Laughter* by Marjorie Holmes. Copyright © 1967 by Marjorie Holmes Mighell. Excerpt from *My Religion* by Helen Keller. Excerpt from *Adventures in Contentment* by David Grayson. Copyright 1907 by Doubleday and Company, Inc. Excerpt from "Orion Rises on the Dune" in *The Outermost House* by Henry Beston. Copyright 1928, by Doubleday and Company, Inc. All reprinted by permission of Doubleday & Company, Inc. Excerpt from *A Gift of Joy* by Helen Hayes with Lewis Funke. Copyright © 1965 by Helen Hayes and Lewis Funke. Published by M. Evans and Company, Inc., New York. Words by Anne Morrow Lindbergh excerpted from an address given at Smith College, copyright © 1970 by Anne Morrow Lindbergh. Reprinted by permission of Harcourt Brace Jovanovich, Inc. Excerpt by Stewart L. Udall from *The Quiet Crisis* by Stewart L. Udall. Holt, Rinehart and Winston, Inc., publishers. Excerpt by Rachel Carson from *Silent Spring*, by Rachel Carson. Copyright © 1962. Reprinted by permission of Houghton Mifflin Company. Excerpt from the book *More in Anger* by Marya Mannes. Copyright, ©, 1958, by Marya Mannes. Excerpt from the book *Onions in the Stew* by Betty MacDonald. Copyright, 1954, © 1955 by Betty MacDonald. Reprinted by permission of J.B. Lippincott Company. Excerpt from *TWO ISLANDS: Grand Manan and Sanibel* by Katharine Scherman. Little, Brown and Company, publishers. Excerpt reprinted with permission of The Macmillan Company from *Speak to the Earth* by William A. Breyfogle. © The Macmillan Company 1961. Excerpt by Francis Kilvert from *Kilvert's Diary*, edited by William Plomer, is reproduced here by permission of Jonathan Cape Ltd., and The Macmillan Company of New York. Excerpt from "Ode to the End of Summer" by Phyllis McGinley from *A Pocketful of Wry*. Copyright 1940, 1959 by Phyllis McGinley. Reprinted by permission of the author. Excerpt by Hermann Hesse, *Siddhartha* translated by Hilda Rosner. Copyright 1951 by New Directions Publishing Corporation. Reprinted by permission of New Directions Publishing Corporation. Excerpt from *New Bottles for New Wine:* Essays by Julian Huxley. © 1957 Julian Huxley. Reprinted by permission of A.D. Peters and Company. "Song of the Rain" from *Tears and Laughter* by Kahlil Gibran. Copyright 1949 by Philosophical Library, Inc. Reprinted by permission. Excerpt by Pogo from *The Earthlovers* Calendar. © 1970 by Walt Kelly. Reprinted by permission. Excerpt from *The Singing Wilderness*, by Sigurd F. Olson. Copyright © 1956 by Sigurd F. Olson. Reprinted by permission of Alfred A. Knopf, Inc. Excerpt reprinted by permission of Charles Scribner's Sons from *The Invisible Pyramid* by Loren Eiseley. Copyright © 1970 Loren Eiseley. Excerpt by Rene Dubos from *Smithsonian*, copyright Smithsonian National Associates, 1971. Reprinted by permission. Excerpt by Joseph Wood Krutch from *Audubon* Magazine (July 1971). Reprinted by permission of *Audubon* Magazine and Mrs. Joseph Wood Krutch. Job 12:7, 8 reprinted by permission of the Cambridge University Press. Published by the Syndics of Cambridge University Press. Excerpt by Senator Edmund Muskie from *A Statement from Senator Muskie* and an excerpt by President Richard M. Nixon from *A Statement from President Nixon* in *Fortune* Magazine (February 1970). From *Editorial: Reconciling Progress with the Quality of Life*. Courtesy of *Fortune* Magazine.

SPEAK TO THE EARTH

"...speak to the earth, and it shall teach thee ...."

Job 12:8

We travel together, passengers on a fragile space ship, dependent on its vulnerable reserve of air and soil; all committed for our safety to its security and peace; preserved from annihilation only by the care, the work, and the love we give our fragile craft.

Adlai Stevenson

4 *Touch the earth, love the earth, honour the earth,*

her plains, her valleys, her hills, and her seas;

rest your spirit in her solitary places.

Henry Beston

Nature is the master decorator, but then she has the finest accessories at her command. Curtains and draperies of silvery mists and rain and multihued clouds; the swags and fringe and vivid accents of leaves. And the rugs she unrolls—floral patterns, the lush green of lawns and pastures, the shimmering gold of the fields, or the deep white fur of glittering snow.

There are no discords in nature. An art teacher once called our attention to the fact that in nature colors cannot clash, as they can on canvas or fabrics. For outdoor light has a quality that blends their native loveliness, whatever the hues. Architects finally discovered that the most beautiful, livable houses are those which allow nature to do much of the decorating through windows which frame the landscape and draw the outdoors in.

Marjorie Holmes

6   The environment is comprehensive and complex. It is the air we breathe, the water we drink, the noise we hear, the buildings, trees, flowers, oceans, lakes, rivers, and open spaces we view and through which we move, and the vehicles which move us. Our every action affects that environment, and through our ability to extend the application of energy and to manipulate the physical world we have magnified our effects on it.

Edmund Muskie

A man can hardly be a beast or a fool alone on a great mountain. There is no company like the grand solemn beautiful hills. They fascinate and grow upon us and one has a feeling and a love for them which one has for nothing else.

Francis Kilvert

There seems always to be something new

to watch on the river, something new

to marvel at in the thickets and the woods.

Helen Hayes

Siddhartha said: "Is it not true, my friend, that the river has very many voices? Has it not the voice of a king, of a warrior, of a bull, of a night bird, of a pregnant woman and a sighing man, and a thousand other voices?"

"It is so," nodded Vasudeva, "the voices of all living creatures are in its voice."

Hermann Hesse

10 I am dotted silver threads dropped from heaven
By the gods. Nature then takes me, to adorn
Her fields and valleys.

I am beautiful pearls, plucked from the
Crown of Ishtar by the daughter of Dawn
To embellish the gardens.

When I cry the hills laugh;
When I humble myself the flowers rejoice;
When I bow, all things are elated.

The field and the cloud are lovers
And between them I am a messenger of mercy.

I quench the thirst of the one;
I cure the ailment of the other.

The voice of thunder declares my arrival;
The rainbow announces my departure.

I am like earthly life, which begins at
The feet of the mad elements and ends
Under the upraised wings of death.

I emerge from the heart of the sea and
Soar with the breeze. When I see a field in
Need, I descend and embrace the flowers and
The trees in a million little ways.

I touch gently at the windows with my
Soft fingers, and my announcement is a
Welcome song. All can hear, but only
The sensitive can understand.

The heat in the air gives birth to me,
But in turn I kill it,
As woman overcomes man with
The strength she takes from him.

I am the sigh of the sea;
The laughter of the field;
The tears of heaven.

So with love—
Sighs from the deep sea of affection;
Laughter from the colorful field of the spirit;
Tears from the endless heaven of memories.

Kahlil Gibran

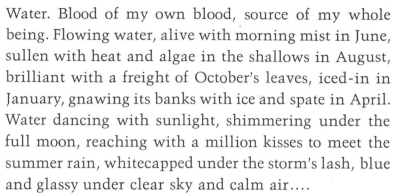

14 *It is the marriage of the soul with Nature that makes the intellect fruitful, and gives birth to imagination.*

Henry David Thoreau

Water. Blood of my own blood, source of my whole being. Flowing water, alive with morning mist in June, sullen with heat and algae in the shallows in August, brilliant with a freight of October's leaves, iced-in in January, gnawing its banks with ice and spate in April. Water dancing with sunlight, shimmering under the full moon, reaching with a million kisses to meet the summer rain, whitecapped under the storm's lash, blue and glassy under clear sky and calm air....

Deny the rivers and you deny the brooks; deny the brooks and you deny the springs. And the springs came from the rain, the rain came from the clouds, the clouds came from the oceans. An endless cycle, water to water, life to life.

It is no one man's story. It is the story of the race. Down from the trees, out from the caves, down to the brookside for the sweet, clean water. Down the brook to the river, keeping to the lush banks where all life, including man, can thrive, down the river to the sea. And you walk in the rain on the beach, the ocean rolling in great combers, sloshing your feet, touching you with the hands of kinship. You walk, you throb with the beat of the waves, you taste the salt on your lips. You find shelter, on an island, and you sleep. And the beat of the past, the ancient beginnings, is like the throb of an echo in a conch shell at your ear. You are a child of the water — the salt, the sweet, the eternal water.

Hal Borland

The West has told its sons: "Take from the earth as you wish, the more the better. Breed as much as you wish, the more the better. Consume what you wish as you wish, the more the better. Build what you wish and where you wish, the more the better. Dominate as many markets and as many people as you wish, the more the better. Make as much profit as you wish, the more the better." The living Planet answers: "Please stop. Turn around. You can't keep on doing any of these things. This isn't addressed to your altruism. Just for you and your children to survive, you'll have to stop grabbing at every natural resource; they are running out."

George B. Leonard

The earth can be an abundant mother if we learn to use her with skill and wisdom — to tend to her wounds, replenish her vitality, and utilize her potentialities.

John F. Kennedy

In 1970 the wounded Apollo 13 swerved homeward, her desperate crew intent, if nothing else availed, upon leaving their ashes on the winds of earth. A love for earth, almost forgotten in man's roving mind, had momentarily reasserted its mastery, a love for the green meadows we have so long taken for granted and desecrated to our cost. Man was born and took shape among earth's leafy shadows. The most poignant thing the astronauts had revealed in their extremity was the nostalgic call still faintly ringing on the winds from the sunflower forest.

Loren Eiseley

Man's mind is a partner with nature. 21

Julian Huxley

(Man) thinks of himself as a creator instead of a user, and this delusion is robbing him, not only of his natural heritage, but perhaps of his future.

Helen Hoover

Man's daily life and his aspirations cannot be thought of apart from natural events because they are the ultimate expressions of our living Earth.

Rene Dubos

A plant is like a self-willed man,

out of whom we can obtain all which we desire,

if we will only treat him his own way.

Johann Wolfgang von Goethe

Water, soil, and the earth's green mantle of plants make up the world that supports the animal life of the earth. Although modern man seldom remembers the fact, he could not exist without the plants that harness the sun's energy and manufacture the basic foodstuffs he depends upon for life.

The earth's vegetation is part of a web of life in which there are intimate and essential relations between plants and the earth, between plants and other plants, between plants and animals. Sometimes we have no choice but to disturb these relationships, but we should do so thoughtfully, with full awareness that what we do may have consequences remote in time and place.

Rachel Carson

It is satisfactory…

to plant things and

have them thrive.

Betty MacDonald

…[I'd like to say that] I'm against the Cherry Tree Myth. The Cherry Tree Myth, as it came to me as a child, had a moral which I took to be: "It's not so bad to cut down the cherry tree as long as you don't *lie* about it." I accepted it once, but I have begun to wonder. I could argue that a lie is usually discovered. It can be admitted and corrected. The cherry tree is gone; and too many of them have been cut down already. I'm for the cherry tree.

Anne Morrow Lindbergh

Summer...this green, this lavish interval,
This time of flowers and fruits,
Of melon ripe along the orchard wall,
Of sun and sails and wrinkled linen suits;
Time when the world seems rather plus than minus....
Phyllis McGinley

We enjoy the lonesome and the empty

because, unlike our ancestors, we are too familiar

with the crowded and the confined.

Joseph Wood Krutch

Beyond all plans and programs, true conservation is ultimately something of the mind—an ideal of men who cherish their past and believe in their future. Our civilization will be measured by its fidelity to this ideal as surely as by its art and poetry and system of justice.

Stewart L. Udall

We have met the enemy and he is us.

Pogo

I have two dogs, a big black German shepherd, and a smaller white hunting dog.

I don't know what price I would place upon these two great animals. Let's say half my income, because they insist that I go out regularly to see the nature of which I am a part. Through them, I've learned about woodchucks and fox and skunk and deer. I am lured by them into winter and summer, into the vast geological history of the land I live on, past old fences that Bucks County farmers built a century ago, and along trails I would not otherwise have known.

More especially, they remind me that I, too, am an animal first and a thinking human being later. And I have come to believe that any living thing is better off when it lives closest to its inherent nature. My dogs know no tricks. I could not imagine one of them rolling to please me. They are animals concerned with rabbits and squirrels and strange smells in the woods, and their fulfillment comes in being animals. When I am with them in the fields, I am a man-animal and it is damned refreshing to be reminded of one's inherent limitations and capacities. I owe these two wonderful mutts a debt that could never be repaid, for they have taught me about myself and my world.

James Michener

Bring out your social remedies!

They will fail, they will fail, every one,

until each man

has his feet somewhere upon the soil.

David Grayson

Man has applied a great deal of his energy in the past to exploring his planet. Now we must make a similar commitment of effort to restoring that planet. Our scientific capacity has grown so much that we are able to leave the earth; yet our glimpse of its beauty from the barren moon has only reminded us of how much we must love earth's qualities.

Richard M. Nixon

A child said What is the grass?

fetching it to me with full hands…

I guess it is the handkerchief of the Lord….

Walt Whitman

Along the brushy path we heard a winter wren sing and stopped to listen. No sound in the world is so joyous, and few birds are heard so seldom. You have to go a long way, quietly, into a deserted forest to hear this shy creature. Warbles and trills, brilliant and high-pitched, continued past belief, like the Emperor's Nightingale, until it seemed the bird must have lost breath. We lost ours in listening.

Katherine Scherman

Even if intelligent man were able to shut out of his active mind the problems that plague us, the so-called advances of modern technology wouldn't leave him many areas of refuge. The jet contrails cross almost all the mountains and forests, and the pollution now washes almost all the beaches.

But for my *attempt* to find the solitude that permits one to think — perhaps, if he's lucky, even to muse — I go to the sea by small boat. With one's vessel propelled by the same power of wind that moved the ancients, faced by the same challenges and beauty of nature, at work or unleashed, one can feel a kinship with all living things and achieve, at least momentarily, some degree of serenity.

Walter Cronkite

Furs look better on their original owners.

Friends of the Earth

The earth we abuse and the living things we kill will, in the end, take their revenge; for in exploiting their presence we are diminishing our future.

Marya Mannes

In the long war on wildlife, man has steadily advanced and wildlife retreated. We are now in danger of achieving total victory. We have the capability to wipe out competing life on a tremendous scale. In such a victory we would surely find catastrophic defeat.

Faith McNulty

To deprive the globe of physical wilderness

would be to give a deep wound to our own kind.

F. Fraser Darling and Noel D. Eichorn

That the sky is brighter than the earth means little unless the earth itself is appreciated and enjoyed. Its beauty loved gives the right to aspire to the radiance of the sunrise and the stars.

Helen Keller

I like trees because they seem more resigned

to the way they have to live than other things do.

Willa Cather

Wind, the greatest force of nature, will be the last element to be tamed by man; for the next few millennia, we must learn to live with it. But scientists are already at work, looking to the future when they will control the weather and eliminate its excesses. There will be no tiresome wind; the bora, the mistral, the simoom and the Santa Ana will be banished to the history books.

Let them think hard before they remove our daily stimulus. For we do not wish to inhabit a spider's web world.

J. A. Maxtone Graham

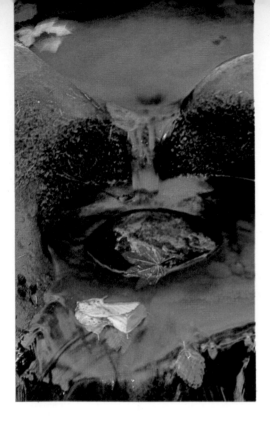

The beauty of our land

is a natural resource.

Its preservation

is linked to the inner prosperity

of the human spirit.

Lyndon B. Johnson

Conservation is a state of harmony between men and land. By land is meant all of the things on, over, or in the earth. Harmony with land is like harmony with a friend; you cannot cherish his right hand and chop off his left. That is to say, you cannot love game and hate predators; you cannot conserve the waters and waste the ranges; you cannot build the forest and mine the farm. The land is one organism. Its parts, like our own parts, compete with each other and cooperate with each other. The competitions are as much a part of the inner workings as the cooperations. You can regulate them — cautiously — but not abolish them.

William A. Breyfogle

Early morning in the wilderness is the time for smells. Before senses have become contaminated with common odors, while they are still aware and receptive, is the time to go hunting. Winnow the morning air before it is adulterated with the winds and the full blaze of sunlight, and, no matter where you happen to be, you will find something worth remembering.

Sigurd Olson

But ask now the beasts, and they shall teach thee;

and the fowls of the air, and they shall tell thee:

Or speak to the earth, and it shall teach thee:

and the fishes of the sea shall declare unto thee.

Job 12:7-8

Man must be able to escape civilization if he is to survive. Some of his greatest needs are for refuges and retreats where he can recapture for a day or a week the primitive conditions of life.

When man worships at the feet of avalanche lilies or discovers the delicacy of the pasqueflower, or finds the faint perfume of the phlox on rocky ridges, he will come to know that the real glories are in God's creations. When he feels the wind blowing through him on a high peak or sleeps under closely matted whitebark pine in an exposed basin, he is apt to find his relation to the universe.

William O. Douglas

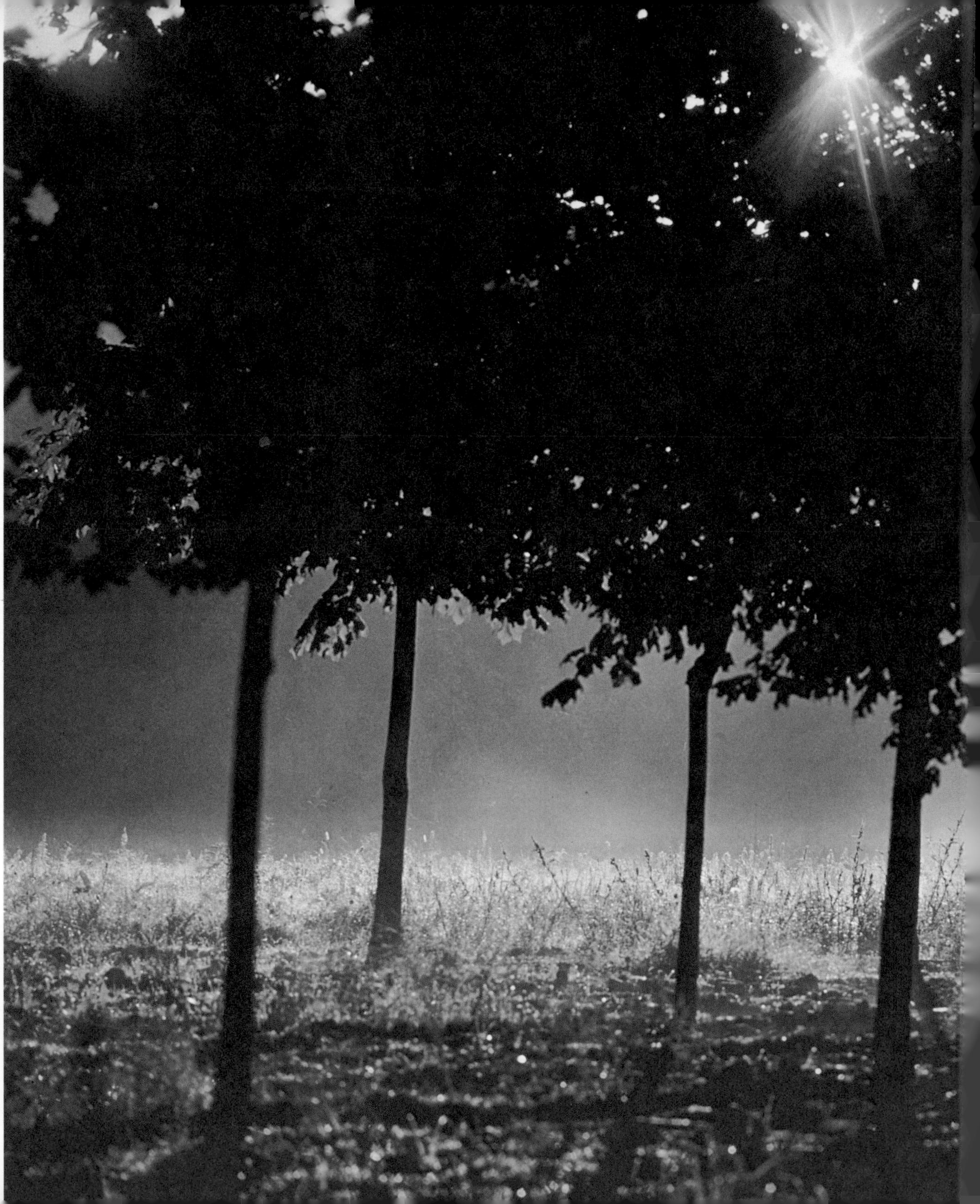

For I have learned
To look on nature, not as in the hour
Of thoughtless youth; but hearing oftentimes
The still, sad music of humanity,
Nor harsh nor grating, though of ample power
To chasten and subdue. And I have felt
A presence that disturbs me with the joy
Of elevated thoughts; a sense sublime
Of something far more deeply interfused,
Whose dwelling is the light of setting suns,
And the round ocean and the living air,
And the blue sky, and in the mind of man;
And motion and a spirit, that impels
All thinking things, all objects of all thought,
And rolls through all things.

William Wordsworth

Photographers

Bernard Blake — Back Endpaper (R). Ron Brown — Front Endpaper (M), Pages 23, 52. Keith Carey — Page 33(B). Color Library International — Pages 5, 35, 47. Allen Corbin — Pages 12-13, 36-37. Arnaud Derosnay — Front Cover. Phoebe Dunn — Front Endpaper (L), Pages 19, 28, 60. Richard F. Fanolio — Pages 32, 54. Carol Hale — Pages 26, 42-43. Carter Hamilton — Front Dust Jacket Flap. Grant Heilman — Pages 17, 24-25, 33(T), 44, 45, 46, 55(L), 58, Back Endpaper (L). Maxine Jacobs — Page 51. Joseph Klemovich — Pages 14, 20-21, 40. James V. Lipp — Pages 9(R), 10-11. C.G. Maxwell — Pages 7, 55(R). Sue Morey — Pages 4, 22, 39. David Muench — Front Endpaper (R), 5(R), 6, 15, 16, 29, 38, 48-49. Joseph Muench — Pages 8, 30, 41, 59. National Aeronautics and Space Administration — Page 3. H. Armstrong Roberts — Title Page. Shostal Associates — Page 53. Ed Simpson — Page 9. Charles Steinhacker — Page 50, Back Endpaper (M). Gary Turner — Pages 56-57. Joe Van Dolah — Page 27. Larry West — Back Cover. Steven Wilson — Page 31. Jack Zehrt — Page 18.

Titles handset in Trump Italic by Volk and Huxley. Text set in Trump Mediaeval by Hallmark Photo Composition. Printed on Hallmark Crown Royale Book paper. Designed by Ronald E. Garman.